SMALL FIRES

///

José Angel Araguz

FUTURECYCLE PRESS
www.futurecycle.org

Library of Congress Control Number: 2017938699

Published by FutureCycle Press
Athens, Georgia, USA

ISBN 978-1-942371-28-1

en memoria de Pedro Araguz Aldape

Contents

section one

section two

section three

section one

Small Fires

the stories of a new world end like this

my grandfather's house at the edge of a landfill

my mouth dry for hours on the road

I knew we were close when traffic split, my mother's knuckles white

my grandfather with his hat in his hands, posing for a photograph

the stories of the conquistadores end like this

my grandfather's gold tooth showing when he smiled, hat in his hands

the turn from highway to gravel, to mud, to where we had to park,
walk the rest of the way

my grandfather's house, the grackles, brushstrokes leaving a painting

dust thick on the truck my mother had bought him, the TV, the fence
she helped build

the train tracks we knelt between and played games

the stories of the Aztecs end like this

newspapers where dead children keep appearing, black and white
on the front page

they looked asleep in the backseat, they would find their stomachs cut,
filled with cocaine

my grandfather's house, the rats ruminating in the sun

the stories of Santa Ana and Pancho Villa end like this

the mesquite trees, the sap dark, the hours I had to look at it

my grandfather's house of cardboard and wood scraps

my grandfather's hair slicked in waves of ash, hat in his hands

the stories of the narcocorridos end like this

a cracked egg in another boy's hand

the beginning of a beak

of an eye opening

stories, not ballads, reveling

my grandfather who beat his daughter and now was dying in clothes
she bought for him

my grandfather's house, the flies, thick words stumbling off the page

stories, not heroes, revising

my grandfather's house in the rain, I asked, got slapped for it,
would it sink or sail away

the mesquite trees we broke twigs from to feed small fires at night

stories, not sacrifice, revisiting

my grandfather's prayers to a ceiling with holes in it

the canals dividing the neighborhood, the stories of the dead

stories, not conquest, reverberating

trains on the tracks, only at night, only in dreams, each car a house
never lived in, passing on

we would talk for hours, until our faces and hands and words
were covered in ash

stories, not a new world, a world made new from what was here

my grandfather's house of rain, when he died, the rain died too

stories I have to tell, my mouth, the road, his hat in his hands

La Llorona at the Border

It is not children she wishes to steal but time,
not a river but distance holds her reflection,
her black hair the sky, tears on her face streaming
into each other, roads on a map that keeps
unfolding. It was not her child she buried that day,
that day that keeps occurring every time
her story's told, not a coffin she stamped
down into the dirt, but a heart. She marked
the spot with her braid, chopped and tied it to
a cross made of twigs, vowed to grow it all back.
Now, her screams scare children, multiply
the shadows in their rooms, become gossip,
like: *I heard she doesn't just steal kids,*
she drowns them, drowns herself every night.
Not a child but a man on the other side
of a river, a man smuggled between milk crates,
sleeping on the concrete floor of where
he has found work, falling asleep each night
to the same dream, his knees knocking against
his chest, the faces of others seen in flashes
of street lamps, his tongue drying to a paper
he has written his name too quickly on.
Not a child but belt buckles left behind,
trucks that rattle like cages, frayed and faded
baseball caps, boots of stretched and hardened
skin. Not a child she keeps searching for
each night she walks, not a river but distance
keeps unfolding her reflection across
a horizon that keeps shifting with each step
she takes towards a border barring nowhere.

Mesquite

One day, a man decided
he could walk across Texas
and grew old trying, lost
his way, ended up twisted,
turned around on himself,
reaching out an arm, then
another, and then another,
until he was only arms
pointing all around
at the horizon—his skin
hardened, but his body began
to snap, and could be picked up
easily by the hands of
children at their games,
pretending at divining
water, writing curses
in the dirt, later
dropping him into
the fire, not all of him,
only a piece, a broken
part of him he knew
would only just grow back,
and he would let it—his heart
burst into sap, a dark
seen through, slugging down
toward feet that have forgotten
where they were going.

Hails from Corpus Christi

I would be belted after dinner,
my food eaten with the moon,
the night a table where a place
is set, and a place diminishes—
hardened, chucked out of the sky,
milk-glow, but a rap like a stone,
the kind in movies thrown at windows
to get someone's attention—I was all
attention as my mother's boyfriend
turned to rain and thunder,
clouds broke into fists and cries
broke the sky of my sleep with lightning
that held fast in me, turned me
into that color—a hardened flash
falling through the years into a room
where I tried to restrain the weather
of what I felt, but raised
my voice, punched the wall, the table,
clawed after and clutched your arm
as you tried to leave before
hearing what I had to say,
clutched and pulled away to see the white
of where the blood had left, a hardened
streak that burst into
your hand hard across my face, your voice
no longer a voice I knew,
a voice that from then on
kept me at a distance,
would harden and check me for years,
distrustful, despite our apologies,

despite tears and my own diminishing
voice, a pebbled voice, a grit,
shit shit shit under my breath
every time we'd argue, knowing
there was nothing I could do
but take it, hold my clouded self,
not wanting to hit, ricochet, scatter.

Midas

After punching the wall—after
she rushes out of the room—in that
silence, remorse starving me down
to tears, I become Midas after:
bathing in the river, carrying
a jug back to the palace, eager
to wash everything back to what
it was, stopping to think of his golden
daughter (the look on her face, would she
speak to him), catching himself
in the light of this water he holds
close (silver, different, precious),
and hoping in time his hands
can set things right.

Frog Meditation

After beatings, I hid
with skin like water
broken at the center, heartbeat
in ripples. I mashed
my child's fist in mud
and closed my eyes. Within my cold
and slithered skin, I swilled
secrets, sputtered every thought.
Willing myself into the dark,
down to the size of a rock,
I strained to hold another's
anger. Pulsing for hours,
I wished to be thrown,
thinking I would hurt nothing
hitting water, only sink
into the color of bruises.
Long after the moon had risen,
I stirred, and added my own gnarred cry
to the others at their practice.

Stitched

Shopping after the accident,
my aunt said: *See anything
you like and we can take it,
just have you mother open
her stomach there,* then pointed
as my mother laughed,
and I recalled the black
smile stitched into
her side, the lines to me
not healing her, holding
her shut instead, like the door
of the hospital room
I was kept out of when
she wasn't awake—the accident
from the other night,
how her boyfriend insisted
that he wasn't drunk
and drove her car into
a tree, how she had felt
safe with him before,
how she really needed that,
looked to each man in her life
for the father she'd lost faith in,
for the man her father failed
to be so early on she
was a child when she left,
how her boyfriend now wouldn't
visit, had come out of the wreck
unharmed while she kept falling

out of herself—all of this needing
to be held in, sewn up
so she would not hurt,
and me then not wanting
to want anything,
so she would not hurt.

Sin

Heavy with the sin my mother spoke about,
from time to time I felt a pig following me
around the house. I'd get brave, swear,
turn my music loud, or take a long look at the neighbor

as she watered her plants, and hear the animal's slop-breath
in rhythm with mine. I never saw him. Even when I tried my mother's
bra on at a mirror, and jumped out of the way, my stamping heart
muffled his hooves stamping off. Now, putting down the phone

after a man growls: *Stay away from my wife—*
or hearing myself say: *I've got a lot of growing up to do;*
after the woman whose bed I'm in reminds me
I have a girlfriend waiting up for me—each dark

turn in the mud of the man I am is confirmed
in the dull clomp of the animal who tramps alongside me.
He grunts with me at being asked: *So what are you—*
South American, or something—

like it's that easy to know just what you are
when what you are is everywhere and nowhere,
is the sound of a chuckle and snort you can't place,
a chortled breath you feel others can hear,

why else the looks of mistrust, of being out of place,
the sound so much, I have grown quiet,
only to hear myself not know
how to avoid becoming more

like the animal that has me cursing under my breath
in two tongues, ripping pages out of Bibles,
always for the same lines: *And I gave my heart*
to know wisdom,

and to know madness and folly,
words I repeat to myself
downing another beer,
having nothing else to offer.

Cazar Means to Hunt Not to Marry

I thought it was a love story, a wedding
taking place in *The Book of Fables,*
the first in Spanish given to me
because I was always reading
(*por eso ojos de vaca,* one aunt
would say), never alone but
as alone as I could get.

I tried to follow the *cazador*
hunting after the fox, but was stopped
by the fox falling on her side, turning
back into a woman; the wailing
man, the *cazador,* also stopped
to hold her in his arms. The ceremony
made no sense. I tucked the book away

with my toys under the sink, and let
the story sit there in the dark,
rooted with the things I'd learn
to leave behind. Like a root,
the story spread in offshoots down
into my life. *Casar,* my mother
would say after hours talking

in a parked car with a man whose face
I'd never see because the porch light
was kept off. *Casar,* she'd say to me
as I grew up and moved from place
to place, asking if I loved my books,
if I thought they'd care for me
as I grew old. *Cazar,* I later read

in another book, another fable,
and saw for the first time
that the word I heard so often
from my mother was cousin
to this other word, that each sounded
the same—*to hunt, to marry*—
How many pages had I turned

and in my own confusion read
violence as love, had read one word
and let the meaning shoot right past me,
an arrow cast for its own sake, without caring
where it hit? How long will the chase
after a woman feel like a chase
away from myself? Will this forever

be the story? Where is the book
I can pull out to go back
to where I started: a man
fumbling his way to a clearing;
a fox stopping, holding still,
silently scanning the sky
for something that has yet to fall.

Quinceañera

The women of the house shook her from sleep,
and began to serenade, trying to mark
the air of another rite that seemed to come

too soon, the song her father should have sung
instead of barking, running her off, a song
with the momentum of a hand ready to skip

a stone across water, a hand which would
fall away soon as the song was done,
but not before a stone danced,

lifting and lifting off the face of water,
each time as if it'd never drop—past midnight,
the women sang, without ceremony,

without food, without a sense of how
to ready a girl to skip into the current
of her life, could only sing,

their voices cracked and strained, trying
not to wake her son who slept beside her,
a son who would grow up and dream of the night

these voices broke the air and raised a song
for the little girl his mother was,
for the woman she now had to become.

Eavesdropping

Let him listen, let
him learn to be a man—
I did not want to hear
the slap and groan,
the wood floor hollow,
a belt buckle thudding
like a dropped flashlight,
did not want to hear
wet leaves sliding
the hum of lullaby
at the back of the throat
rising, yes, rising—
But he's right there,
he's right there—
my ears burning,
my mother's name now
forgotten, her face falling
through the walls, contorted,
terrible, God on her lips—
I closed my eyes as I would
on every other night
with every other face,
lost in long hair,
drowned in perfume,
(to have hands
heavy on a woman
is to have my ear against
the wall again) where I would
reach out in the black and hope

to pull us apart, to give
us back our faces, sing
us back our voices,
to say: *I'm right here,
I'm right here.*

Kiss

It looks like a kiss, one of those that land
at the end of a letter, proof that a woman still
has lips and wants you to remember. That's why
the lady across the counter smirks and tries
not to laugh. She thinks I rushed out the door
and was pulled back, that I was in a hurry
so a girl missed her mark and smudged goodbye
across my cheek. She thinks it's a badge and me
boastful, slick with affection, or just too
busy to bother with: What? This?
She is not my teeth, nor the ache when I chew my gum.
She is not the woman asking what I mean
when I say I'm a grown-ass man, just who do I think
I have to be. She is not Corpus Christi, its bars
of men, where if you don't have a woman on your arm
you must be hitting on theirs. She is not the voice
I ignore while I point at my tattoo, my dead
father's initials on my calf, and say:
See, if it's important enough I'll bleed.
She is not the bottle smashed across the side
of my head, harder than a fist, I heard it
shatter into: Hey, I'm talking to you.
She is not my elbows as I steady and brace myself:
He will hit me again, I should be ready to
explain it away to my little brother.
She is not the swelling that starts instantly,
nor the blood from a cut on my brow I feel as though
I must be crying, the way it runs down
my face. She is not me in the parking lot

barking at the friend who knew the guy: Yes,
I was stupid, so was he. She is not
the same friend later who drags his arms
over me, nor the sound of his tongue across
my cheek, rough against the grain. She is still
smiling. I say: You should see the other guy,
he looks a lot better. That's when the lips
she saw on my cheek get lost, become scratches
on flesh. When she says the meal's on the house,
I notice the light move across the lines
of her mouth as she smiles. I catch myself
back in her eyes, my face smaller, somewhere
I've never been, somewhere I haven't seen,
that glimmers and holds, like a wound closing.

As Birds Do

I once saw a man in church kneel
to look his son in the eye and tell him:
You have to be quiet now, God can hear you,
his finger skyward, in the direction
of the crucifix. The boy's eyes,
as if it were a just-learned word,
widened, as if making room,
as if each time the broken body
was seen anew, everything—this life,
the life around it—was made new.

      *

After the fight, I cringe when I see
another man. The bruise in the mirror
I press my finger to is the size
of a fist not raised, a blow not returned,
of a door I drew once in a book,
bearing down on my pen, thinking
I could bring King Arthur back
to help me do battle with the man
beating my mother, her bruises,
doors that never opened.

      *

I have had to study manhood
like birds study the rain, have had
to read the same sentence over
as screams went on in other rooms,
have gone around bruised, saying:
Dogs get hit like I got hit,
and been the only one to laugh,
have let the seasons tell me where
to live, but never how to get there,
nor what to do during a storm.

El Río

The river, like a dream, keeps changing,
pixelated in a soap opera
that throws love in the water,
lets it float and turn, reflecting
a woman's face, my mother there

chuckling in the dream each time
someone shouts *ila migra!* explaining
the bogeyman of restaurants
where at a moment's notice
you had to be ready to catch fire,

to drop and roll—keeps changing
across the gleam of sunglasses
and badges where I see myself
reflected in the backseat, a child,
hiding how scared I am

by keeping my eyes wide,
cold waters rising, stinging,
I feel the whole sky could fall in—
keeps changing in the dream,
walking with my mother

down a street she's never been on,
talking of California, how people
have no more luck than frogs
dashing across the interstate,
a river of cars coursing,

leaving people to be dragged off
like driftwood—keeps changing
around my mother's shoulders,

mosquitoes bristling across her neck,
her ponytail black and shining

with sunlight one moment,
with moonlight the next—like a dream,
keeps changing, I feel the waters pull
when storeowners see me and freeze,
become those paintings on the wall

with eyes that follow your every move—
the river, like a dream—the drag
when I'm pulled over and it takes
three cop cars to do it,
my name, coughed in static,

read off my license with the grace
of a beer can crunched underfoot—
the river, like a dream, keeps—
my mother shaking her head,
saying there were no breaks,

no sweeping violins,
no rescuing lover in a jeep—
like a dream—*Cuando viene
la migra, vienen lágrimas,*
she says again,

and wipes what could be light
from her face.

Alien

When I heard this word first thrown around
in conversation, my family's Spanish
cracked to let in this strange stretch
of cautious whisper, the weather changed
in my mind. I'd read of spaceships,
of planets so advanced you could
travel freely, no stopping to be
asked about citizenship, no stone
face behind a badge peering
to where I sat in the backseat.
The world became another place.
The word *wetback* began to bring
to mind the scene where the dark creature
burst from a woman's stomach
in a movie. The sky grew overcast
in my mother's eyes, kept her inside,
when someone talked of borders.
Rosaries turned secret communicators.
Prayers: reports of worry and want.
Each crucifix, a satellite.
Before, I would stand outside and look
at what I felt to be not empty space
but an open window to another life.
Now, another life invaded.
There were people with papers,
and there were people without.
There were questions I was told
the answers to should they come up.

There were stories I was asked
to forget. When my mother pressed
the silver face of St. Jude
into my palm, I felt the weight
of it, the cold and unfamiliar
feel of what I didn't know.

The Name

for Pedro Araguz Aldape

Asked where the name comes from, I grow quiet,
and in another voice begin to tell
how those ending in *z* are from the Moors
who ruled Spain 800 years. Some agree,
read into my black hair and dark skin
what they wish to. I let the disguise of story
take over, let it pass across the feeling
in my chest that tells me I've lied, even
when I haven't. A name is wind and ink,
a name is memory. What does it matter?

        *

What does it matter my mother didn't want
my father in my life, even in name,
and reached out to her father for his?
Who remembers that, and who can clearly
tell it, when Mexicans stack up last names
like a trail of crumbs behind a person,
syllables broken off a whole to meet
and make another whole, a map of breath
drawn over so one can't get lost. Eventually,
everything gets lost. What does it matter?

        *

What does it matter letters and sounds hold,
become a space where the lost young man I am
can look and catch a part of the old man
my grandfather became? What does it matter,
except that I remain and have to face

the name, have to explain it, give it meaning:
the name, the house at the edge of a landfill,
the hat held in his hands as we talked, the wind
leaving behind a faceless and fleeting sound.
Asked where the name comes from, I grow quiet.

Luchadores

after Cathy Park Hong

They were the only men in the house,
and stood firm, one hand raised
saying farewell, the other idle.
I'd make each bed, wash dishes,
set chairs back in place, then dig
under the sink where their masked faces
waited to be pulled out. I fought
with them all afternoon, took turns
playing villain, playing good,
letting each one win, then starting
over. The light in the garage apartment
turned all summer, flickered
light and dark across the floor
as on the leaves outside.

La Llorona at the Café

She used to sit down and tell
stories about the river.
Her hands would shake.

Her cup and saucer made up
the background to her words.
She never spilt.

Once, she said: *You can't hold
water in a fist.*
We liked that,

so much, we kept repeating it
to one another,
missed when she left

the room, back to the river.
At night, we hear her shake.
Hear the girls

rattling dishes, the boys
stirring sugar around
in empty cups.

section two

The Accordion Heart

The accordion heart is hard to carry.
There are no hands for it. To play,
you go from face to face and wait
to see who wakes it up. You'll feel
the air inside you pull and stretch.
You'll feel awkward and loud, and yet
each movement could be music. You
can see where this could lead to something.

Sometimes the face won't want to play.
Sometimes the face will play too long.
Either way, you'll feel worn out.
You'll want to punch and tear a hole,
and prove the accordion heart is useless.
There are no hands for it. You wait.

Autumn Walk

On my walk, bits
of dry leaves mix
with gravel. I hear
the click of bracelets,
the costume jewelry
she'd wear to be
adorned. Leaves
change color, and I see
the wigs she wore to work.
Leaves fall, and I hear
the arguments we had,
the arguments we swore
we'd never have, the river
colored by the muck
below, by the sky
above—feel each memory
mix with gravel,
down to the last
fireflies, the light enough
to keep me looking
long after they're gone.

Divorce Suite

I.

I could start with the summer we moved to a new city, not even a year into the relationship. We sat on the porch steps listening to trains pass in the distance.

I could say one train was leaving.

Beside me, the woman I would marry, then leave, was showing me the scars she made from cutting herself. Her favorite: inner thigh, grub-white lines: something digging itself out. I imagined her hand against herself, a hand wanting to see how skin opens and closes like a door, scars like light around the cracks.

Someone in there who will curse me. Someone who will tell me she wants to give me a reason to call the cops. Someone who will want to beat me like I was beaten as a child. Someone who will throw whatever is in her hand. Someone who will throw stuffed animals, picture frames, a jewelry box. Everything hitting against the walls like someone knocking, banging, slamming themselves against a door.

> Hard breath at the hinge of a scar.
> Scar like a keyhole to a person.
> She told me she felt cold
> doing what she did.
> I said nothing.

I could say one train had just paused, was changing tracks.

I could say I knew the names of every passenger on the train, their destinations, their thoughts as the sun went down in the window frame where they had watched the miles pass like water.

None of it would be enough, none of it would be everything.

There will always be what she heard, what she would say.

I will start with the cicada husk on the railing that evening. When it swayed, its whole body said: no song.

II.

The first Christmas she scowled that I had not proposed, her face multiplied on the ornaments shaking on the tree. Her steps that morning could have shaken down the stars.

When I first met her father, he sat next to me and never looked over, only kept checking his watch and glaring at his wife and daughter. He, too, was not expecting any of this. When we had first moved, he called and said not to get his daughter pregnant. This was a month into not having sex, which became years. I reassured him I always had condoms. He could only meet my eye when drunk. Now that's family, I felt. He had a swagger talking to me then, as if on a dare to himself. Once, he showed me his fishing lures in the garage, his dartboard, the holes his aim could make. The day of the wedding, her father took me for a walk, talked on about responsibility. I kept thinking she had his eyes, the gray broken exactly like gravel.

On the last night of the wives, there was one who favored fire, who punched her palm and said she wanted to give me a reason to call the cops. One who shrieked, feeling hunted, and one who shrieked, feeling wrong. One answered to the name of a slammed door. The one I walked out on spoke to me as though she'd cough her heart right out. Were I to make for the door, one would scream. Were I to stay any longer, one would scream.

After a time, our home became simply the space where we ate and took turns waiting for the other to leave so that each could undress and whittle away at their body alone.

I knew it was bad when I grabbed
the jacket of the girl I worked with
in the backroom,
held it close to my face
and breathed in.

The Christmas I did propose, she laughed, the sound like someone
unfolding a map, the kind you quickly open wide to see where to go,
and know right away you won't be able to fold it back up.

    III.

if not, winter: words from Sappho engraved on the ring I threw into
the river.

Afterwards, where the ring had been: a white band, absence looped
around my finger, a motionless strip, I had to wait it out.

When I think of her now, my breathing changes: not the panic
of then, more the play of air moving around a cat batting down and
eating moths.

Towards the end, I found myself staring at the walls from time to time.
She had insisted on painting them the last summer, said it would be
good for us. When I moved out, I braced under boxes for hours. At one
point, I slipped and caught myself on a wall with one hand. Under my
hand, an unevenness: two flies stuck under the paint.

    I'm leaving and I'm sorry.
    I'm leaving and I'm sorry.
    I'm leaving and I'm sorry.

What was each word said but a cloak shared between two in bad
weather, fought over, wrestled free by one, then the other—we lived
together listening to the sound of that fabric tussle, enduring the storm.

I had to wait it out.
Sunlight at the edge of blinds.
Scar where she cut herself: grub-white.

IV.

Inside me, a turn like the wrong ends of two magnets: a pushing away:
two dark things refusing this side of themselves with no power over
the other.

Flipping through photographs, myself as curling creature to child at
his mother's side, eyes wide on the first day of school, to young man
standing at a distance from his own wedding, in the spot where his
family would be had they attended, young man standing, eyes low,
where they would have met his mother's had she been there at his side:
the face I was, changing, a candle burning in reverse, coming together
from the bottom to what stands in the eyes here: flame, less than flame,
cold wick fraying.

I used to write a poem a day for her. When I go over the poems now
I find they are not about her but another woman, one made up entirely
of beginnings.

Outside of an abandoned house in the new city, the creak of a door
inside could be heard from the sidewalk. The wind would come hard
over the river, would try to push me aside, but I would linger, not
wanting to get home, only wanting to listen to the sound: something
opening, something closing.

> The cage of lost sleep:
> the moon looked in
> to see itself
> broken in two
> across my eyes.

The last morning we woke up together, I didn't know it for what it was. All the plans, the words, rehearsed and in me: what to do with them, and how and when—I mistook the silence in which these questions left me for just another morning. An unmade bed. A light breaking in at the edges of the blinds.

Some nights she would hand me a book, tell me when her mother read to her she would fall asleep with all the characters still at their beginnings, nothing lost, no one hurt, a world where people were simply ideas, then lay back in bed, leaving me with an open book, in charge of telling her how the story ended.

V.

In the Book of Hell, I stop on the giant mouth swallowing a crowd of people while an angel holds a key to the side of the jaws, a look on the angel's face like the one I might have had sitting across from her, explaining I would be leaving, a look of not knowing if there was something opening or something closing, a look of not looking away.

> What I remember of that night
> is not her face or what she said
> but the silver gleam
> off the brooch she wore made from a coin
> passed from hand to hand in another life.

I blinked and saw her one day as one sees stones at the bottom of a stream: dark, distant, and clear.

> *Dissolution:* this other word on the forms,
> marriage a thing that can disappear
> like salt tossed in a broth.

I didn't cheat—I knew things were different. It's all about fine lines.
As soon as I knew things were different I let her know. On paper,
it will look like I cheated. Fine lines: the paperwork was not in yet.
I knew things were fine lines I had to sign, had to have her sign.
She and I not married a full year: fine lines: when I say five years
it is the sum of the life together. I didn't cheat, I was cheated.
ImleavingandImsorryImleavingandImsorryImleavingandIm

When it rains, I remember the bedroom covered in clothes where
a woman had taken off every mood and color and stormed away,
behind her a quiet where the cold earth snaps like fire.

Sewing needles gleamed as I turned on the light and began to sift
through broken plates, cut-up condoms, pieces of a broken clock.
A thin, white glare flickered in and out, a sort of lightning as I cleared
a path through what she had left me: a mess radiant like rain.

     VI.

There is an old German custom where a tree is cut down and set aside
for a bride and groom to saw through together in order for them to learn
if they can cooperate. I like to imagine the moment before the first cut,
when both are convinced of being capable, and both are doubtful.
Each with a hand in the work that will show them for what they are.

She hated to hear me eat. Insisted on the radio, the television,
something to drown out the sound. With my mouth, I argued. With my
teeth, I ate my shame. The heart is an awful teacher: it moves like a
mouth, but says little. All the time, little.

The wedding party consisted of the ex's father, brother, and sister—
her mother officiating—and me. My mother's take on the wedding:
Me tragué mi corazón.

I read that drowning is not what one would think of it: a flailing of the arms, a gasp, a cry for help, but rather a silence, the lung's primary purpose being breath, there would be nothing for the voice to come alive with, any cries or calls would be cut short by the body's instinct to keep the heart going.

I waited almost a month before calling my mother. Between losing sleep and changing apartments, there was no time. When I say time, I mean nerve. When I did call, my mother seemed relieved. She said she knew it took time to leave a bad relationship. She said with time I would feel better. That she always knew when she was in an abusive relationship there would be other times, times to move on, times to be happy, times to say *love* to one's self. She had never spoken directly about those times. Then, she only had time to say someone was leaving before quickly closing the door. Through those brief cracks of the door, her cracked voice closing.

> The heart is a thing in motion,
> like the stars, like the ocean.

My aunt's take on the divorce: *El corazón no se manda,* only she said it regretfully, as if she would have it otherwise, as if her heart had left and she would order it to come back.

In an email from her mother: *One day she'll be thankful for this. What a tragedy that you did become just another poor, mexican man from corpus christi with no real future. Your mother must be so ashamed. I know I would be.*

VII.

When a relationship ends, certain words begin to taste of winter, taste of seeking warmth.

Kali, the destroyer, she called me her *Kali.*

Even the first gestures carried the air of misdirection. Fingers held together and rising to an open mouth first meant not that one is eating or has, but that one wants to.

There was the Halloween she painted her face the black and white of a calavera. *Like Dia de Las Muertas!* she kept explaining enthusiastically to people, over and over mispronouncing the day of remembering the dead as the day of dead women. I was afraid to correct her.

She would talk about my skin, how it looked against hers, that she would want skin like that. *We would make the cutest brown babies: your curly hair, your skin, my eyes.*

Man up, she'd say, after: *Why don't you—, You need to—*

Language is learned and carried like a shared belief, yours and not yours, open to interpretation, to change depending on need and want. Like air becomes your breath, and leaves you to return to air. With each word, we speak the language of misdirection.

Inattention, ruin, disrepair, taste of just before.

I forget when she stopped calling me her Mexican boyfriend, thought of it only later when she growled at the end, said she would try and have me deported.

> *Abandon*
> could start a fire
> in winter—
> I say it once,
> and savor.

Misdirection has me here holding dry leaves gathered from the corners of the apartment we once shared, the cold making my teeth meet and meet, as if about to speak, but forgetting and forgetting. This feeling now of dirt between my fingers: I no longer give it a name.

VIII.

One year exactly since I married one woman I found myself deep in the woods with another, thrusting and slipping into the undergrowth and bracken, and saw myself for what I was: a fire striking itself alive.

The hunter in stories asked to take the envied, inconvenient child off into the woods and kill them always stays his hand and lets them go as if knowing his part in the story. Doing so frees him, makes a space in him where he can measure himself in the continued footsteps of this other. How long does he listen to those footsteps, how long until they are no longer a sound in his life?

> I hear the tango defined
> as a sad thought one can dance,
> and try to imagine what it would be like:
> all I can see is my shadow.

Instead of goodbye, she tells me about the fish who fell in love with the bird, how it could find no answer to the question of where they would live, and so began to cry, her tears rising, rippling the surface of the water. The bird had no idea what went on, only figured something stirred beyond what he could know, leaving him looking at himself differently, no choice but to fly away.

Lethe

My face and neck dripping
with water, I stood before
the bathroom mirror in
a convenience store, hoping
to wash away the scent
of this other woman
I did not want found out,
not until I knew
just what she was to me,
what story to put her in
for the wife I'd yet to leave,
for the wife I felt I couldn't,
not until I traced
the other's scent around
my skin, to distinguish,
to make sure—the water
hit, the water cleared,
the water left me
the reflection of
a man smiling,
forgetting in a second
what it was I tried
to hide, and why hide it,
who would drive me to
these waters, and what man
had I been, so wrongfully,
ruinously been,
I laughed at him now,
a different man
behind the eyes

crowned by stray hair,
locked and gleaming
against my skin,
inky letters I knew
I'd have to learn to read.

The After

Was once a foot in snow,
a dark outline, the edge
of a torn letter, I wish
I could go back and make
the pages hold together,
read again the words,
in their meaning warming
to my eyes until
familiar, once familiar,
forgotten, the crisp white
gleam of the words first
read, and then the after,
the way I walk to keep
warm, how this works
for me in winter but fails
the more I walk away
from us, no longer us,
once familiar, forgotten,
the crisp white glow
of snow and breath, the words
if not winter engraved
on the wedding ring
I flung into the river,
wanting *not,* praying
not, the winter of
another life, a dark
outline, the edge
of a torn letter I keep
tearing with each step

because I am a word
and must keep moving,
a word I hadn't read
clearly, a word like any
trying to hitch a ride
to the head, a word, I get on
by foot, the crisp white
gleam read clearly,
and then the after,
wanting, praying,
living, the after.

section three

La Llorona Watches the Movie 'Troy'

She watches Brad Pitt leap, then land a stab
like a hammer blow down. Spends time taking in
the bronze skin of the actors; the way they say 'grass'

like 'toss,' *¡Todo British!* She snags popcorn
by the handful watching the gods
be shrugged off by warriors. During the scene

where the Greeks scurry from the Trojan horse,
their shadows fingers pulling at string
and unraveling the night, her breath is sand

and crackling flame. When they run towards fire
in the desert, towards collapsing roofs
and digitized screaming, the montage

of faces, of bodies pushing against each other,
has her whispering to no one in particular:
¡Mira Baghdad, mira Juárez! and no one

in particular hears her over the Dolby
of swords being unsheathed. She begins to hum,
letting her voice hit the same notes

as the opera singer overlaid during the carnage.
Should anyone look over, they'd see
the silhouette of a woman in the third row

treating the forty-foot screen like an altar.
When, after seeing the toppling of statues
and the scavenging through offerings

to Apollo, sun god, the one who sees everything,
the aged and fallen king staggers in defeat
and cries out: *Have you no honor!*

Have you no honor!, she gasps and nods,
as if watching a telenovela unfold
according to how she would want it. Truth is,

she has seen this all before, has drowned
the brown bodies, has plucked gold coins
from river water before any boatman

could make his way to her. She knows
the blonde and blue-eyed have arrived
to play both hero and love interest again,

that though Helen here is a vagabond Marilyn,
she used to have *un poquito de chile*
in her blood, *y un puñado de lodo*

in her heart. That's why it's a woman
who says: *If killing is your only talent,*
then it is your curse, and says it

like one slapping their hand against the river,
a sting in their hands for a while. Truth is,
there will always be a Brad to leap, and hit hard,

the thud through the speakers like a heartbeat.

Joe

Back in Texas, I was Joe, not José,
my buddies too afraid of the accent
that stood out like a sweat drop
on the brow of a spooked é.
You'd be spooked too if sound
could make an umbrella of your throat

with just one word. With English, the throat
grinds gravel in its shadows. Say *José*
and feel the billow and bloom of sound,
a scissors' snip as the tongue slides, that accent
now a curl on a shaggy-haired é,
jet black and waiting to drop.

My friends were ready to drop
classes or pick up teachers by the throat
in Spanish class and fill the room with their gasping 'e-e-e!'
All to avoid saying words like *porque* or *José,*
as in—*Por qué José no tiene* accent?
But that's exactly what I mean! That sound,

that Tex-Mex, Spanglish, barefoot in the mud sound.
It was enough to make me want the sun to drop
from the sky; in the dark, my skin would accent
nothing. I could live in that black where the throat
swallows tears, drown the José
in me, reclaim and silence that é

that stares back from the page, that é
questioning me with its cocked eyebrow. No sound
sleep in that house where even my mom didn't know José

It's Joe, Mom, not José! and I wouldn't let it drop
until the bird of her voice died in her throat,
all for Joe, dark syllable without accent—

Joe, who went to the land without accent—
college—Joe, who never dropped *E*
but swallowed oceans down his brown throat
straight from brown bottles, who bobbed, blinked at the sound
of glass thudding—Joe, who let his mother's call drop
with her crackling voice asking for not-quite-José—

when *Joe* leaves her throat now, I am lost to the sound.
Each accent is the sound of force, that é
would take flight, not drop. *It's me, Mom, José.*

Of Breaking

Set a bucket down,
and eventually the water
will stop breaking.

Until then, only points
and cuts, light breaking
on the surface.

I sit along the sea wall,
would see my face break
if I sat closer.

As the light breaks, there is
darkness, too, breaking,
along the edge.

After a while, faces
appear, shift on the water,
faces breaking.

There are steps, as though
I could walk into
the water and break.

As though I could walk down,
gather the breaking faces,
and hear them speak.

As though I could ask
and get an answer: *Who set you
down to break?*

Until then, silence, points
and cuts, light breaking,
darkness, too.

The Things to Fight Against

for Selena

Onstage, mouth brimming with the Spanish
parents teased her with, maybe she looked
down and saw the cowboy hats, the boots
     and belt buckles, the purses, curls,
and children, maybe she saw herself,

thought: Of all the things to fight against,
sound's not one of them—sound of applause,
sound of gritos, sound of sparked cuetes,
     sound of beer cans gasping open,
sound of buses turning in the dark,

groaning in dreams, sound of Rs rolling,
sound of birdwing flutter, sound of wind
over open water, sound of flags
     unfurling, sound of flame flaring
up and out of a struck match, sound of

a voice, my own Spanish unsure, chopped,
shaky, sound of a bullet breaking
through the air, sound of a newspaper
     splayed on the wind, the news floating,
punched with the grace of long hair—her hair

now a cold blade of bronze, her statue
along the sea wall, to see her is
to see the tide forever turning,
     pulled and pulling away, is to
think again of her killer, crying

in her car in a stand-off, gripping
the gun which would later be broken
to pieces and thrown into the same
    waters the statue looks over,
is to hear my aunt again call us

a city of crabs in a bucket,
each of us clambering to get out
has another behind them—their face
    similar, a face we've grown with
and understand—dragging them back down.

Performer

On Chartres Street, I admire the Living Statues.
At every word called out to them, I check
the lines of their faces to see if they have changed.
This one in gold is good, is most like stone
and seems to never hear what's being said.
His glow is like the glow I had around me,
instead of a street, a fire on a ranch,
instead of camera flash, a flashed command:
Habla inglés. This was after midnight,
when the adults had drunk enough and started singing.
The other kids would push me and a girl
close to the fire and tease: *Habla inglés,
ella quiere.* Shoulder to shoulder with her—
I must've known her name, but that word
was not important then, that word held still
so others could be summoned—I couldn't see
her face. Laughter broke as the crowd called out:
Di novia, di amor, di boda y flores.
Their laughter was the sound of expectation,
a sound like the coursing of a fountain,
which is the sound of water made to move
and fall and fall over itself, a sound
I heard again when older and alone
with a girl who had just finished asking
for me to speak in Spanish: *Say something
beautiful*—her name, how we met, her love
of being in the room as I spoke to family—
all of it fell as I focused on the glow
of the candle I had lit for her, having
learned how to set the mood from watching

movies where this kind of thing would never
stop the hero, a hero who would have
done more than just sit there silent, my face
unmoving—I had hardened it to stone,
waited until she walked away, as the crowds
here walk away, but didn't know what would
happen after, how stone comes back to life—
I never learned to collect my heart like the hat
left at the feet of this man so good
at playing stone, laid out for anyone
to drop what they can spare.

Smoke Meditation

At school, I walked slowly,
let others run ahead,
let their voices rise
around me, heckle or call,
question, then leave me alone.

I had family do the same:
run to greet, question,
and snap at my silence,
marking it as what I learned
on the other side.

I couldn't tell which side
along the river the words
dropped off, where my voice—
air pushed, air patterned—
snagged on clouds and stars.

Fire, what is started after
something is struck enough
it begins to strike itself,
does its work in silence.
What crackles, breaks: small talk.

What fire turns out,
flings: idle pieces
of where it came from,
pushed, patterned,
for a while, into cloud.

My voice was clouds along the river.
My voice here strikes itself out,
works in silence. What rises
tastes like ash. A river courses
whatever side I'm on.

Pushed, patterned, I keep
moving, far, a child
at the end of a cloud.
Questions and laughter settle.

Meditation on White Hair

The tally kept in lines
across my body, I grow
old, different. The marks

of chalk on the walls,
my father's prison cell
as I imagine it,

what I've become. That
he kept count by striking
white, fixing it

in place—that it meant
what the moon does
again, snarling through

black clouds—that like
the moon he begins
to piece himself together

in another life—white
hair grows, and seems
stranded, breath pluming,

root-white and reaching
out from me into
the waters of this life.

The Music Inside

Tenía la música por dentro.
Talking about the kind of man
my father was, my mother grows
silent, perhaps recalling
how it felt to pull off his shirt
and find a line of eighth notes rising
from a treble clef tangle of hair.

I know I've grown with the same hair
across my body, around words rising
in silence, know he'd give his shirt
to help, but didn't know his calling:
that like a seashell hardens and grows
to hold the sea, so could a man
call to a woman from something inside.

The Private Life

Private lives play tricks on us: like dragonflies over water
and in high grass, we take turns wading in our own colors,
and evading them. Am I the red, white, and other color of

one country, or the red, white, and other of another? An eagle
flies for both. I've flown a reckless path. I feel a border within
myself, and cannot cross to say a word without leaving others

behind, cannot cross *ausencia* without nights of walking alone
cold in a new city, unable to look the angel in the eye
who reached from the passenger's seat and steadied

the car my mother let veer, held the wheel and hoped
the jolt enough to wake her up in time, angel whose wings left
stitches and a memory she cannot place, angel who has me believing

my mother and father passed each other one last time despite
being in two different countries, while I spent afternoons
listening to doors open and close from inside the hospital chapel

where I tried to pray but could not say *Our Father* without leaving
mi padre behind, words I never say without some hesitation,
not knowing who they meant and if they'd be heard, words

that a week later became part of a story (my father died in prison
the same week my mother crashed, as if God could only carry one)
a darkness in the chapel nothing could take flight in,

the story hatched its words in us, and those words keep forming
questions: *What is the point of revealing your feelings
without revealing who you are?* But who am I—a resemblance,

a signifier, a connotation in the air of a shared name. From here,
it could be an eagle cutting through the air as I walk in the high grass.
Distance makes a bird any bird, articulates only a dark sliver,

the bend and fold of wings like ink marking a page, a moustache,
my father in a photo, young, with my mother, the separate colors
of their faces, in them already who I will be. The shadows there

between them are my colors. What they will never say to one another
is my private life. When I speak of them—maybe then
the air better known, maybe then iridescence.

My Father's Tattoo

When his body took its
last turn which way
did the tattoo face,
the one with my name,
his name, on his calf?
Which way does the page
of his skin rest?
Who read it?
I am letters on skin,
a repetition,
a page I have
written pages about
because one can read
and read
and still not know.
Not knowing is
a different silence,
one where oceans turn,
and the horizon fills
with barbwire glints—
father of a turning page,
father of ink—here on
my skin the words rise
again, different. I
feel it all different.

My Brother's Ink

for Lupe

I.

My brother covers himself
    in ink. What it means:
    the way skin scars, cleans
and clears what it was, a self
written into a new self.
    He would keep this close:
    his latest, almost
a face, the shape of a son

            he almost knew, skull
            made up of colors,
            made up of flowers
            almost, a name full
            of almost below:
            son he named *Pablo*.

II.

He did not tell me until
    much later. After
    the name picked. After
the name lost. What that small will
meant to him, I can see it
    in the ink still fresh
    in the photo's flash.
When he did call to share it,

            our talk started small:
            work, weather. His voice
            broke into the voice
            I knew once as small
            and full of questions,
            now big with questions.

Blade

Was she flirting with me, this woman that claimed
she only expected three things from men:
to be strong, quiet, and to carry a blade.
I tried to talk again about her homework.
She said of all the men she'd ever met
I talked the most. My being paid to do so
didn't factor in for her. When I asked
if her son walked around with a blade,
she asked if I had ever driven with
my mother past a church. I knew what she
was getting at: the passing of hand and words,
the sign of the cross, the need to feel protected.

*

A rosary or this, back pocket charm
heavy as a rock in my hand. A rosary
or this, steel that unknuckles into lightning.
Each at this hour with the gleam of moonlight and tears.
Each in the hand tallies the night, the shadows gripped
and turned over on each breath. Like a man
refusing grace, I'm silent. Like a man who has found
the whispers taught in childhood to be distracting,
I focus, forget everything but the pressure
of metal that never fully warms against my palm,
and only trust a fist against the fisted world,
my hand closed tonight around this cold peace.

*

I've been told: never pull out your blade
except to use it. If the other guy
has made up his mind, you might as well throw
your wallet at his feet. Me, I've opened
boxes at work, cut roses for my girl,
whittled off the thorns. Even peeled

an orange once. Each time, I felt clumsy,
and wielded the thing like I would a girl's hand
in high school: could never just grip,
had to keep treading the creases, each line
and bump called and recalled, unsure, almost,
if what I felt was really there.

Our Lady

To hear my aunt tell it:
a flash of lightning struck
and stuck firm on the highway,
somewhere between Matamoros
and Corpus Christi, and before
she could know to stop,
she drove past Our Lady
of Guadalupe as she
would've any hitchhiker,
signpost, or mesquite.
This is the gist of it.
What I never get right
when I set myself down
to fix the lightning
by which she saw what
she'd never call a vision,
is how she speaks of it
as if it were a robbery,
with the suspicious
and lamenting tone
of one convinced
something is missing
from her life.

Meditation on the Seconds

My childhood was dust motes seen only in light
I had to come upon: the leaves outside
on summer afternoons, thick light turning
        on the wind: on the way to her eye,

my mother's liner brush, a waiting dab
of light at the edge of so much dark:
Corpus Christi Bay seen from the highest
        curve of the expressway at night,

headed towards what I knew then as home
after having been in Mexico
visiting what my family once knew
        as home, the lights on the water

sparks and glints that left me dark unto
myself. I felt I was only real in moments
of passing light, and had but seconds of
        a life—the lone street lamp

in the park, the fireflies' to and fro—that dust
is made of so much falling gone unnoticed—
the train's spotlight fixed across the tracks—
        little seen of what's ahead.

Night Sky Manifesto

Blueprints I will learn to read.
A stretch of self-portrait: my smile
as a child standing at a mirror
too long. The tinkered lights ships
are lost and guided by. Each mile,
the distance further starred, the course
that should be taken keeps changing.
There is no corner to this, only
nerve: I try to own the sky
and collapse. How it feels to have
my hands in empty pockets. Blueprints
to a house made up of the bones
under my face. Where to begin,
on what level, on what foundation?
Blueprints made on paper that won't
stop moving. What I would see
if I let the river fill my lungs:
my skin could tell my stories, my heart
would cease and fill the sky. Tonight,
a stretch of stars, the knuckles of
a hand, I can't tell what
it offers. I just want to touch
the paper, push against a star.
Skin, tell my stories. Heart, fill the sky.

La Llorona at the Saloon

There are no more dances there.
When she clocks in,
the batwings sound

as if they are ready to drop.
She lays the silver down
and watches faces

melt off the backs of spoons.
Then she crosses herself,
clears her throat,

places the moon at the window.
Some nights, a moth
drifts towards it

and rests on the glass.
Moth legs,
directionless,

slowly turn, soothe
the gray face
with its body.

Canicas

Asked the word
in English, I spoke,
and the other boys
didn't like the sound
of *marbles,*

and I agreed,
not knowing why,
and see now
this other word
had more in it

of the glass clack
and clatter of
those afternoons
where questions
and laughter rose

from the dirt
we kneeled on
into the sky
where any bird
might have

looked down
mid-flight and seen
a formation of boys
shoot beads of light
between them.

Snow in Corpus Christi

December 24, 2004

Tonight, they ski on the beach, build
snowmen with arms of mesquite. Neighbors
walk out on the road, stand there
looking at the same sky, smiling,

finally having something to say.
The snow shapes hills and caves out of
gutted cars parked across lawns.
The man pissing on his neighbor's

roses blinks mid-stream, thinks
revenge, swift and cold, has iced
over his pick-up. The waves foam
in the same color falling down,

the world all ocean· the tide goes out,
leaves me in its wake. The woman
coming out of the club now
has to admit her skirt's too short,

her heels higher than she thought,
the world colder than she left it.
Some call it a miracle. Some
a sign of the end. Some have started

talking about it, and have yet to stop.

On Being Called Jorge

I imagine a city where names,
like taxis, are interchangeable,
a place where Jorge, Juan, and Javier,
and every other man I am
pass each other on the street
and smile, aware that they are one.
I see it for myself: Jorge
in a café crying, Juan handing him
a tissue, Javier slamming his book,
asking them to keep it down.
Tomorrow, you can be Jorge. Tomorrow,
you can be Juan, Javier—whoever
you think I am. Tonight, I am you
blindly in love with what's in a name.

Acknowledgments

Special thanks to the editors of the following publications where the poems noted were published:

The 2River View: "La Llorona at the Café"
Apple Valley Review: "Our Lady," "Canicas"
Asterix Journal: "Asterisms": "La Llorona at the Saloon"
Borderlands: Texas Poetry Review: "My Brother's Ink"
Carve Magazine: "Hails from Corpus Christi"
Crab Creek Review: "Kiss," "El Río," "Alien," "My Father's Tattoo"
december magazine: "Cazar Means to Hunt Not Marry"
Foothill: "The Accordion Heart"
The Indianola Review: "On Being Called Jorge"
The Inflectionist Review: "The Music Inside," "Night Sky Manifesto"
Iron Horse Literary Review: "The Private Life"
Luna Luna: "Quinceañera"
New South: "The Divorce Suite"
North American Review: "Stitched"
Pilgrimage: "As Birds Do," "Smoke Meditation"
Puerto del Sol: "Meditation on White Hair"
Raleigh Review: "Sin"
RHINO Poetry: "Joe" (2015 Editor's Poetry Prize winner)
Switchgrass Review: "La Llorona at the Border," "The Things to Fight Against"
Toe Good Poetry: "Of Breaking"
Waxwing: "Mesquite" "Luchadores"

The poems in section two of this manuscript are part of the chapbook, *The Divorce Suite* (Red Bird Chapbooks, 2016).

The poem, "Blade," was selected by Carl Phillips for a 2016 Academy of American Poets University & College Poetry Prize and published on the Poets.org site.

The question in "The Private Life" (*What is the point of revealing your feelings without revealing who you are?*) is a quote from "Soliloquies With Strangers," an essay from Danielle Cadena Deulen's book *The Riots* (University of Georgia Press).

A warm thanks to Danielle Cadena Deulen for guidance and an early read on this project. A warm thanks as well to Sarah Cortez for including an early draft of the poem, "Small Fires," in her anthology, *Goodbye Mexico: Poems of Remembrance,* whose call for submissions prompted me to begin digging into the material that became this project.

Cover artwork and author photo by Andrea Schreiber; cover and interior book design by Diane Kistner; Georgia text and Futura titling

About FutureCycle Press

FutureCycle Press is dedicated to publishing lasting English-language poetry books, chapbooks, and anthologies in both print-on-demand and Kindle ebook formats. Founded in 2007 by long-time independent editor/publishers and partners Diane Kistner and Robert S. King, the press incorporated as a nonprofit in 2012. A number of our editors are distinguished poets and writers in their own right, and we have been actively involved in the small press movement going back to the early seventies.

The FutureCycle Poetry Book Prize and honorarium is awarded annually for the best full-length volume of poetry we publish in a calendar year. Introduced in 2013, our Good Works projects are anthologies devoted to issues of universal significance, with all proceeds donated to a related worthy cause. Our Selected Poems series highlights contemporary poets with a substantial body of work to their credit; with this series we strive to resurrect work that has had limited distribution and is now out of print.

We are dedicated to giving all of the authors we publish the care their work deserves, making our catalog of titles the most diverse and distinguished it can be, and paying forward any earnings to fund more great books.

We've learned a few things about independent publishing over the years. We've also evolved a unique, resilient publishing model that allows us to focus mainly on vetting and preserving for posterity poetry collections of exceptional quality without becoming overwhelmed with bookkeeping and mailing, fundraising activities, or taxing editorial and production "bubbles." To find out more about what we are doing, come see us at www.futurecycle.org.

The FutureCycle Poetry Book Prize

All full-length volumes of poetry published by FutureCycle Press in a given calendar year are considered for the annual FutureCycle Poetry Book Prize. This allows us to consider each submission on its own merits, outside of the context of a contest. Too, the judges see the finished book, which will have benefitted from the beautiful book design and strong editorial gloss we are famous for.

The book ranked the best in judging is announced as the prize-winner in the subsequent year. There is no fixed monetary award; instead, the winning poet receives an honorarium of 20% of the total net royalties from all poetry books and chapbooks the press sold online in the year the winning book was published. The winner is also accorded the honor of being on the panel of judges for the next year's competition; all judges receive copies of all contending books to keep for their personal library.

www.ingramcontent.com/pod-product-compliance
Lightning Source LLC
Chambersburg PA
CBHW070041110426
42741CB00036B/3125